또박 또박 영어쓰기 단어 100

This **book** belongs to:

Mirae ⓝ 아이세움

알파벳 쓰기

- 알파벳은 A부터 Z까지 26글자예요.

- 모든 알파벳은 대문자와 소문자 두 가지로 쓸 수 있어요.
  우리는 대문자와 소문자를 각각 연습해 볼 거예요.

- 각 글자의 모양과 쓰는 순서를 잘 보고 또박또박 써 보아요.

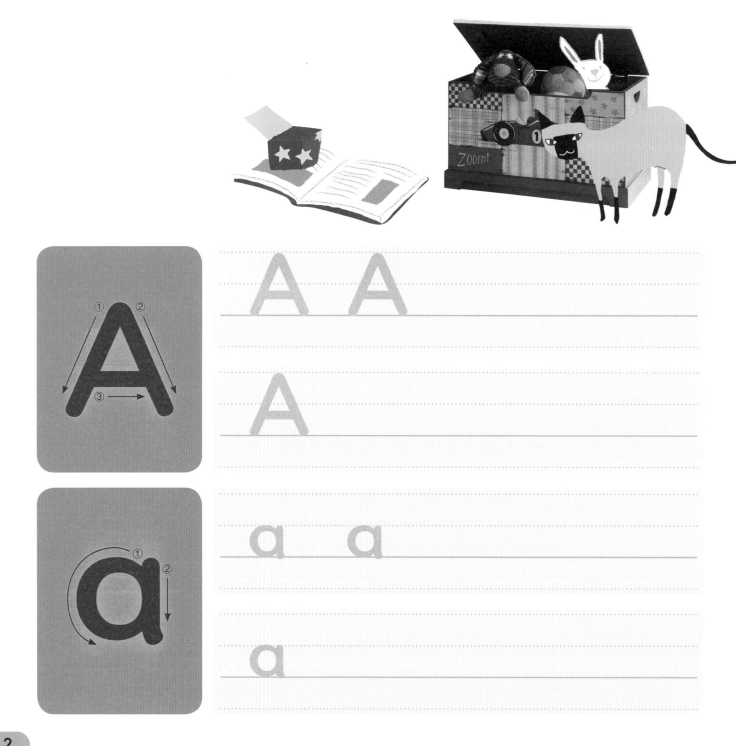

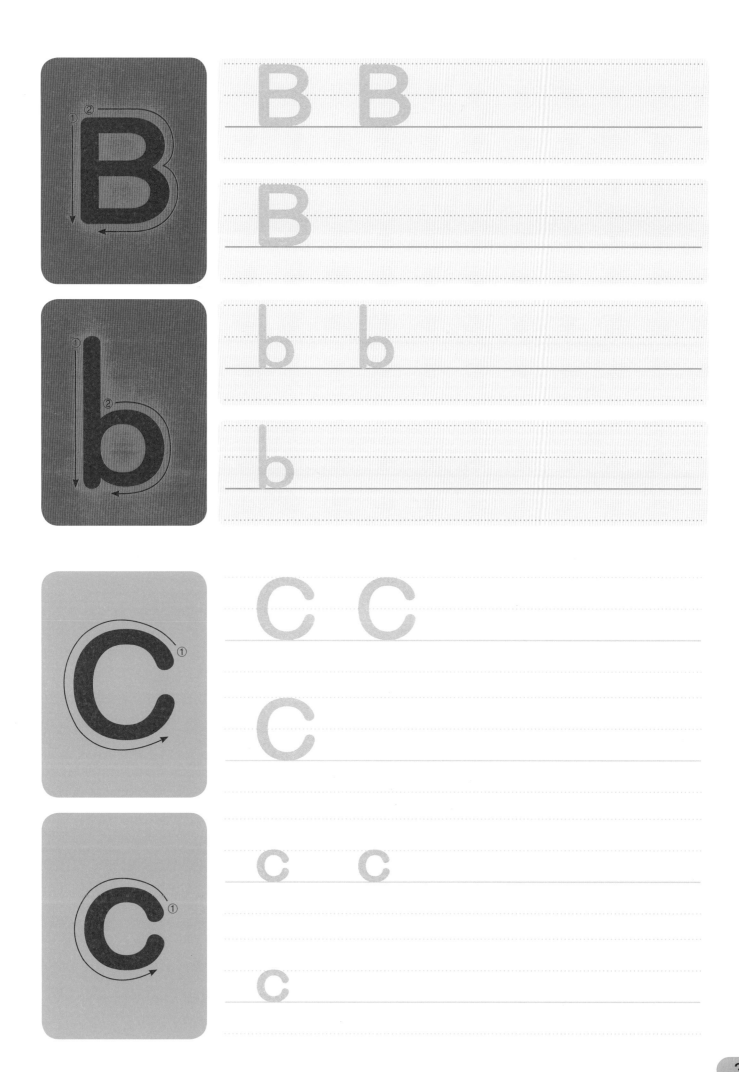

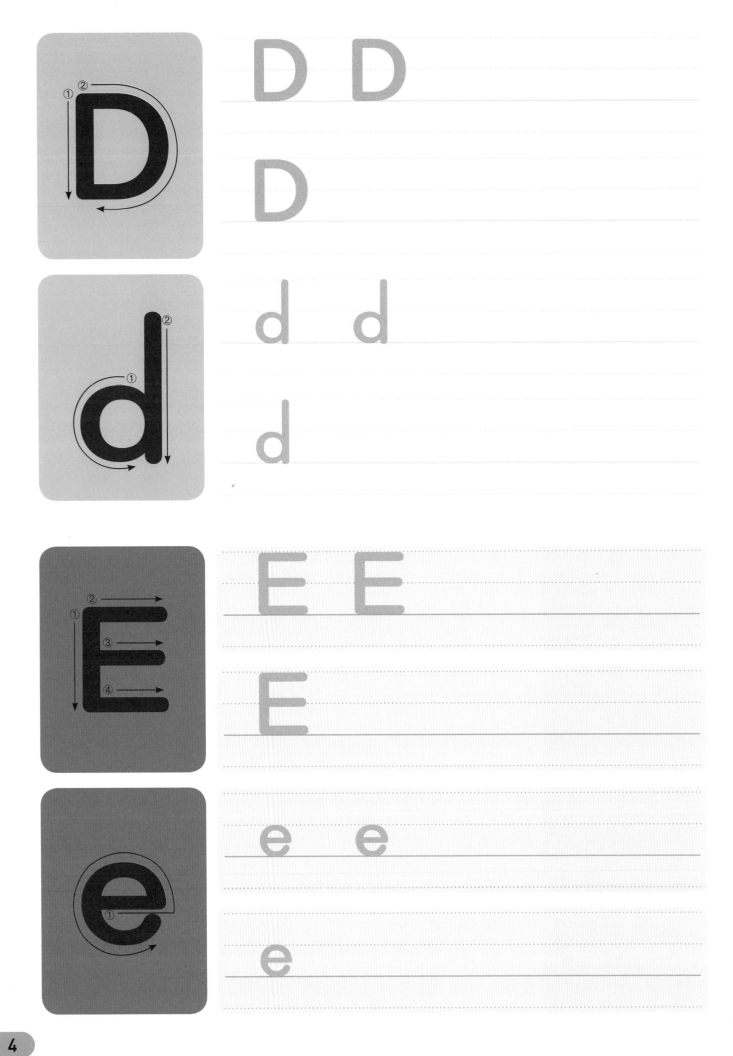

D D

D

d d

d

E E

E

e e

e

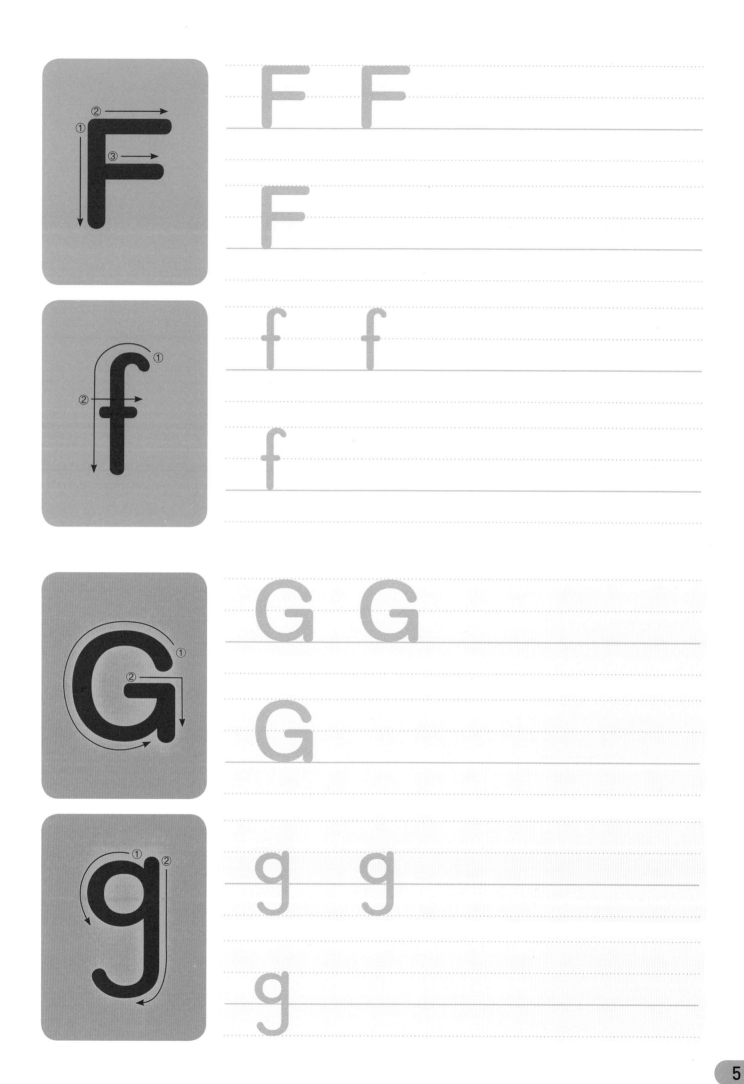

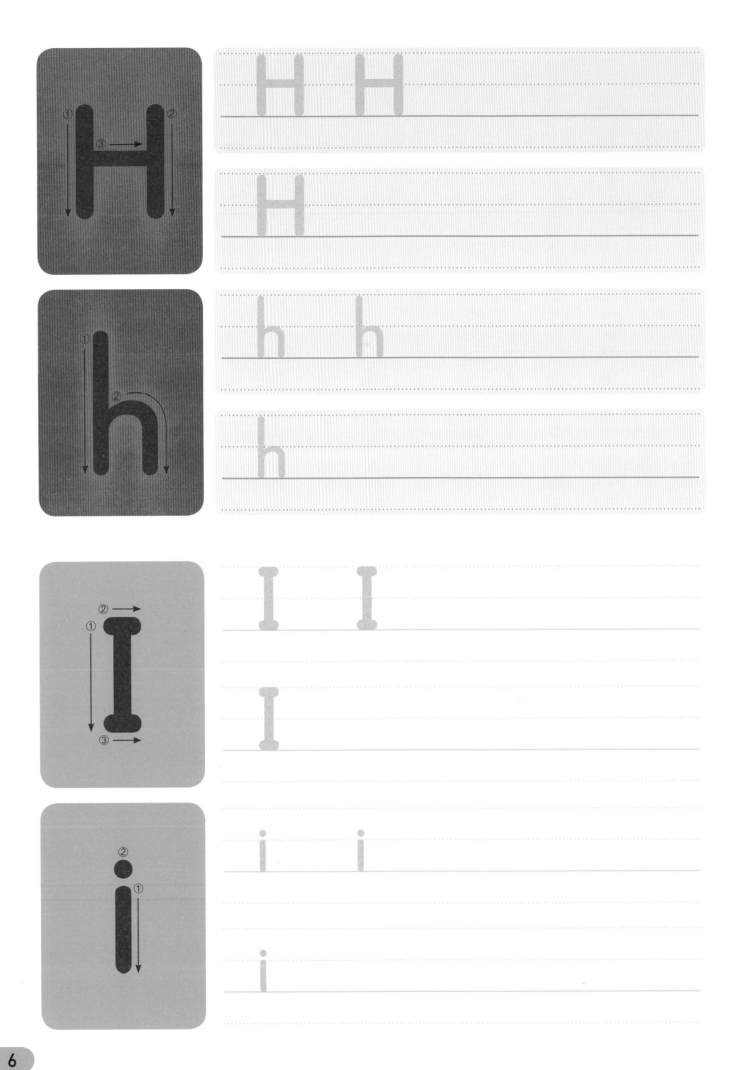

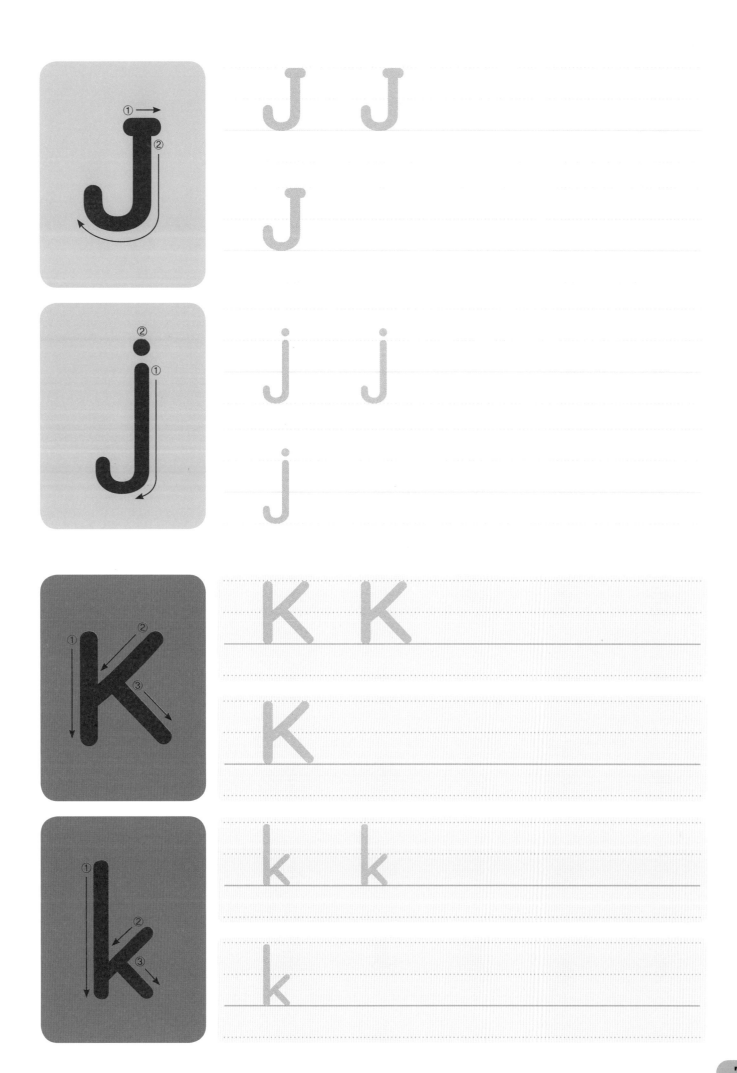

J J

J

j j

j

K K

K

k k

k

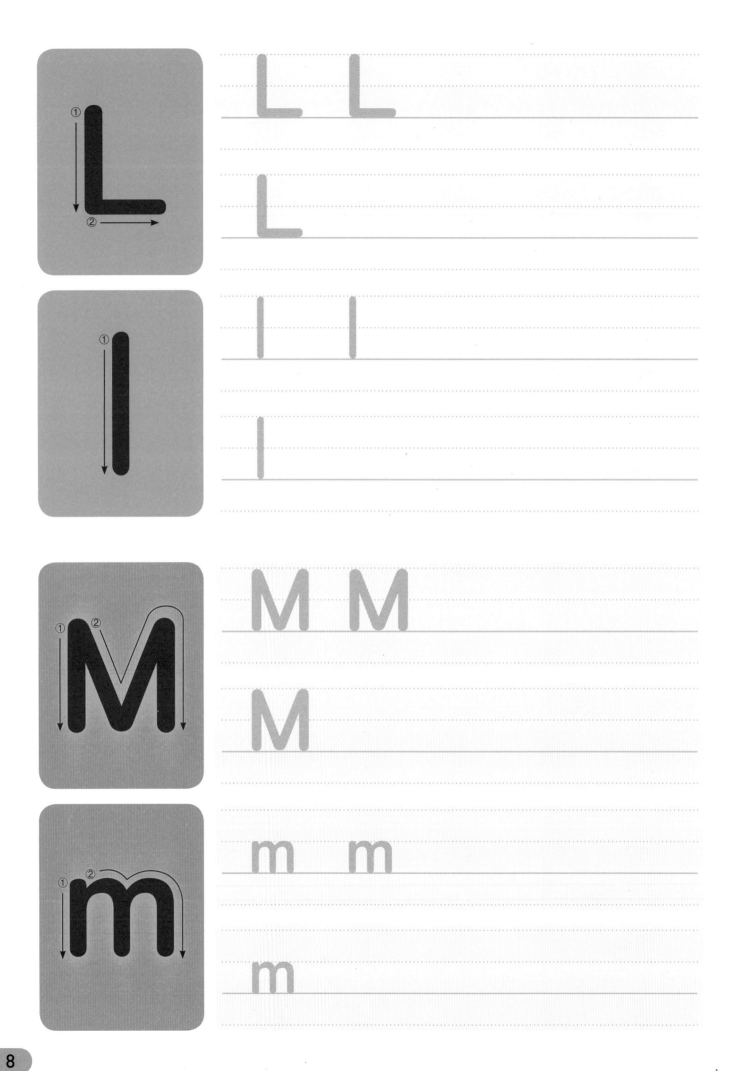

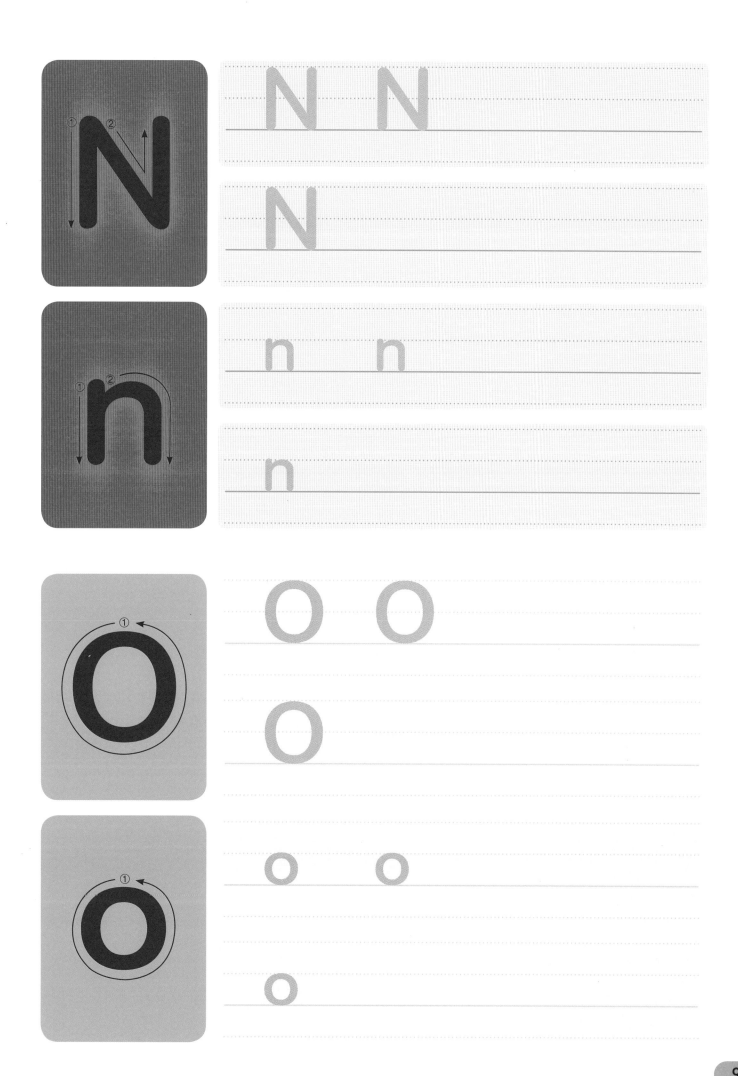

N N

N

n n

n

O O

O

o o

o

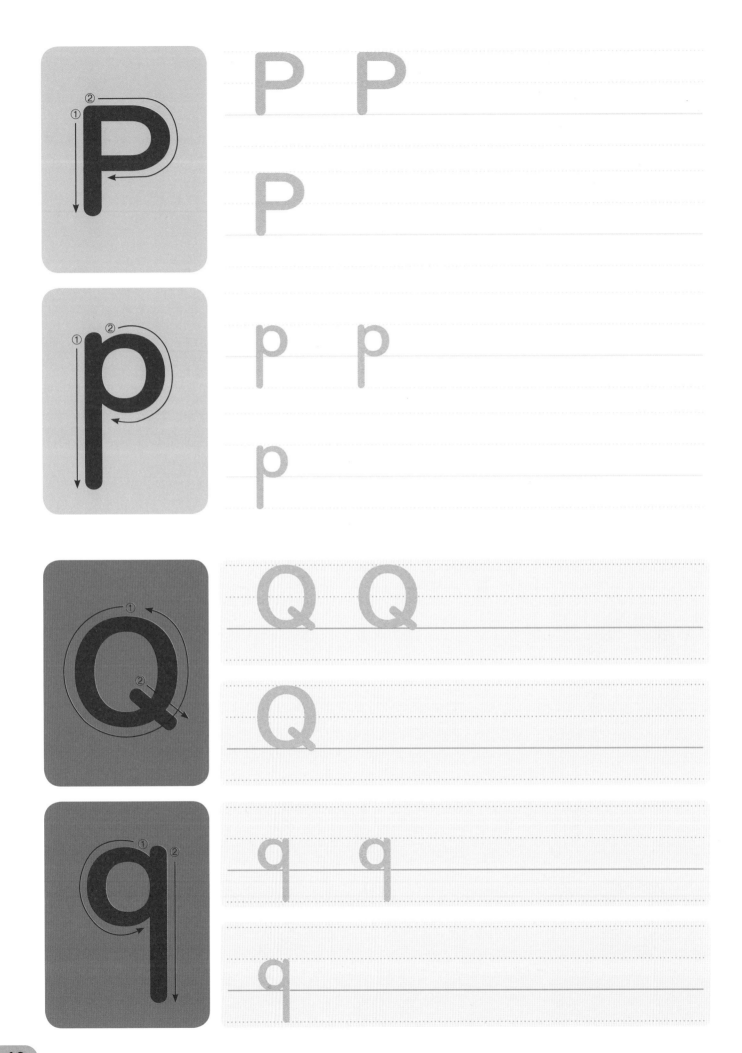

P   P   P

P

p   p   p

p

Q   Q   Q

Q

q   q   q

q

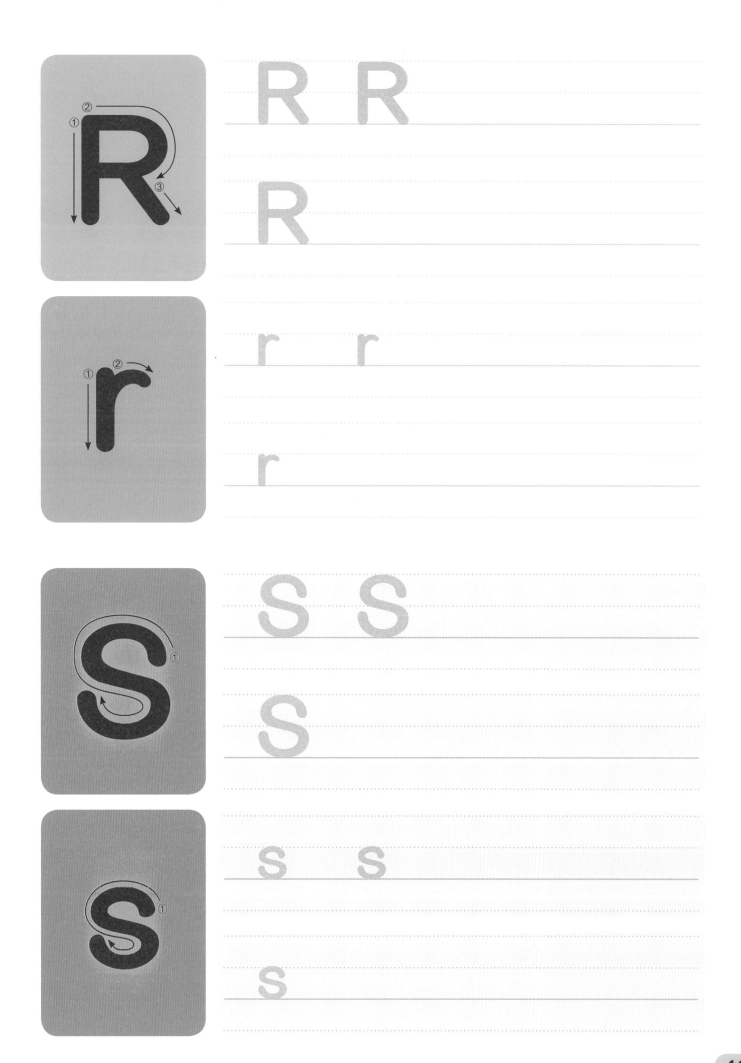

R R

R

r r

r

S S

S

s s

s

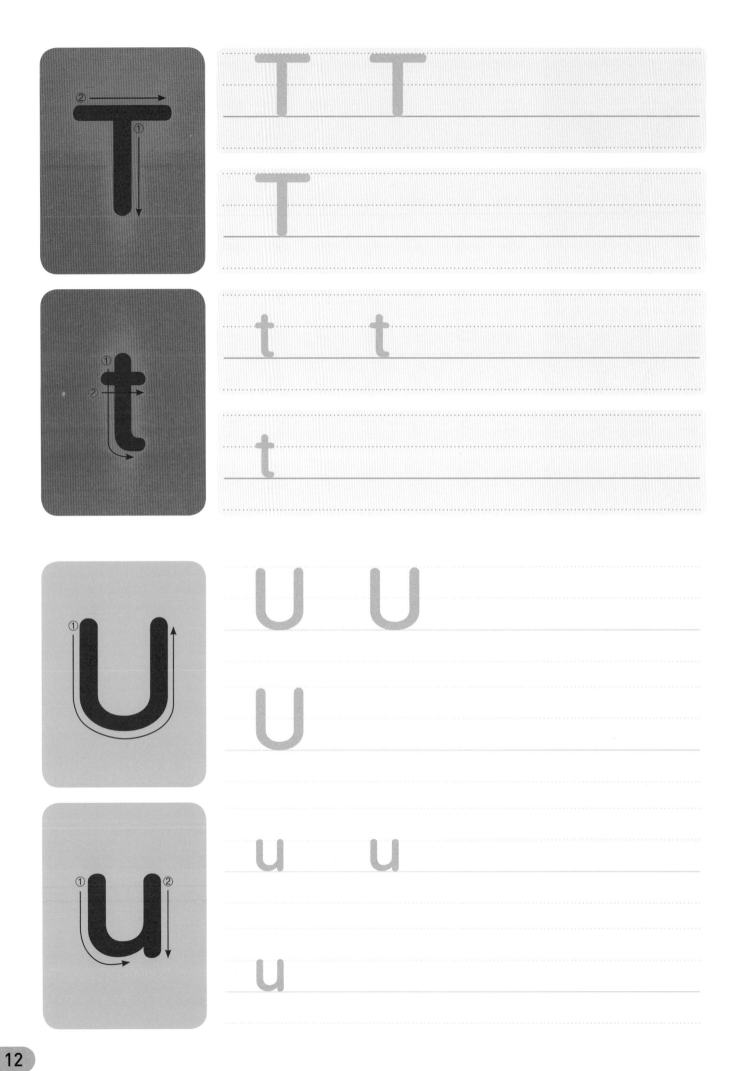

T T

T

t t

t

U U

U

u u

u

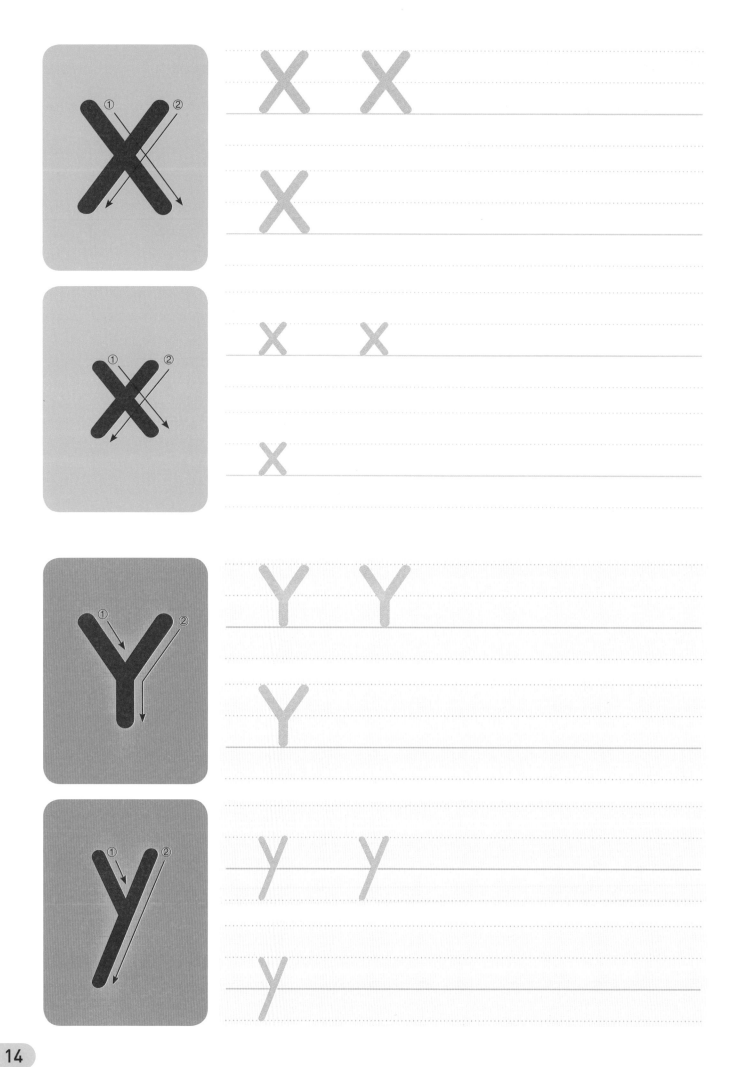

X X

X

x x

x

Y Y

Y

y y

y

Aa Bb Cc Dd Ee Ff Gg

Hh Ii Jj Kk Ll Mm Nn Oo

Pp Qq Rr Ss Tt Uu Vv

Ww Xx Yy Zz

B C A

I Can Be Anything!

• Match the pictures with words!

photographer   teacher   architect   cook   dentist

Write and Read

cook, teacher, doctor, farmer, singer, dentist, photographer, dancer, architect, writer, scientist, firefighter, designer, astronaut

● ● ● ● ●

● ● ● ● ●

singer　　**writer**　　**astronaut**　　**scientist**　　**dancer**

COOKs make good dishes.

cook cook

A Little Talk — I am making food for you. For me? How sweet!

Teachers teach students.

Doctors cure patients.

A Little Talk

😊 I feel sick, mom.

👩 Let's go see a doctor.

😊 Do I have to?

👩 Yes, doctors can make you feel better.

Farmers grow plants.

farmer

farmer

A Little Talk

Who grow plants?

Farmers do.

What else do they do?

They raise farm animals, too.

Singers can sing well.

singer

singer

A Little Talk

Who can be singers?
People who can sing well.
I can sing well!
Then you can be a singer!

Dentists take care of teeth.

dentist

dentist

A Little Talk

Do I have to see a dentist?

Yes, you have a cavity.

Do dentists take care of teeth?

Yes. It won't hurt.

Photographers take photos.

photographer

photographer

😊 I will take a photo of you. 😊 You are a good photographer.

Dancers warm up before dancing.

dancer

dancer

A Little Talk

- Let me dance for you.
- Okay! Go ahead.
- How was it?
- You are a great dancer.

25

Architects design buildings.

architect

architect

A Little Talk

Who designed those buildings?

Architects did.

Writers write stories.

- I am a writer. I can write stories.
- Yes, I read your story once.
- Did you like it?
- I thought it was fantastic.

Scientists do experiments.

scientist

scientist

A Little Talk — What do scientists do? They find out new facts.

Firefighters put out fires.

firefighter

firefighter

Designers create new designs.

designer

designer

  I designed my skateboard. Wow! You should be a designer.

Astronauts
explore space.

astronaut

astronaut

Give Me A Ride!

● Match the pictures with words!

car   taxi   ambulance   train   helicopter

Write and Read

bicycle, car, truck, taxi, bus, ambulance, train, boat, helicopter, airplane, ship, spaceship

truck   bus   airplane   boat   spaceship

I can ride a **bicycle**.

bicycle

bicycle

A Little Talk

Can you ride a bicycle?

No, I can't. Can you?

Yes, I can ride a bicycle.

That's good. Can you teach me how to ride?

34

I want a fancy **car**.

A Little Talk

What car do you want?
I want a fancy car!
What color do you want?
I want a red car!

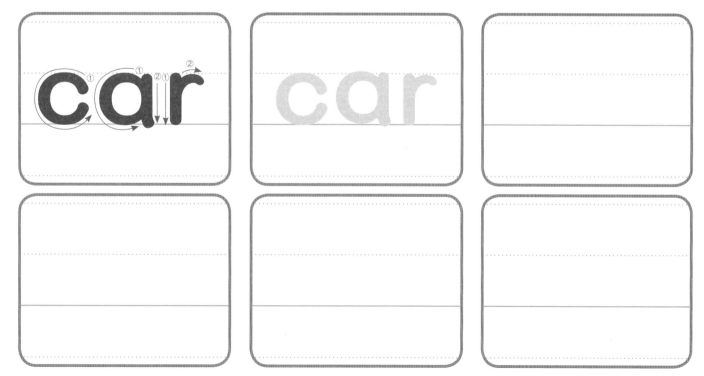

car

car

There is a big truck.

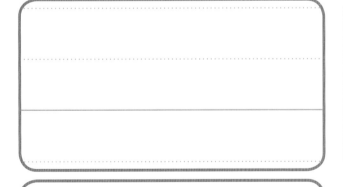

A Little Talk

There is a big truck.
Yes, it is really big.
What does it carry inside?
Probably food!

Taxis are yellow.

A Little Talk

The road is very busy.
It must be rush hour.
Taxis are yellow in this city.
Oh, yes, they are!

taxi

taxi

We will take a **bus**.

Where are we going?

We are going to the mall.

How can we get there?

We will take a bus.

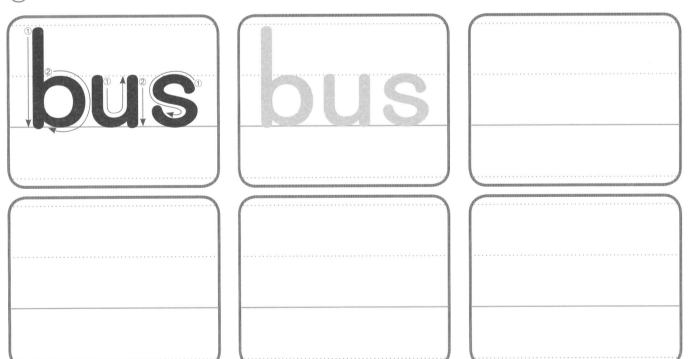

AMBULANCE ONLY

ambulance

ambulance

 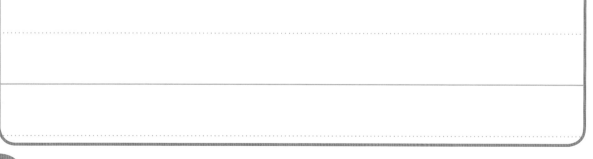

There comes the **train**.

train

train

A Little Talk · There comes the train. · Let's say "All aboard!"

A **boat** ride is fun!

boat

boat

A Little Talk — Do you want a boat ride? Yes! A boat ride is fun!

Look at the helicopter!

helicopter

helicopter

A Little Talk —  Look at the helicopter! Yes. It makes a loud noise.

An **airplane** is in the sky.

airplane

airplane

 Look! An airplane is flying in the sky. I want to fly like that, too!

It is a beautiful ship.

ship

ship

A Little Talk — What is that on the water? It is a beautiful ship.

I want to ride in a spaceship.

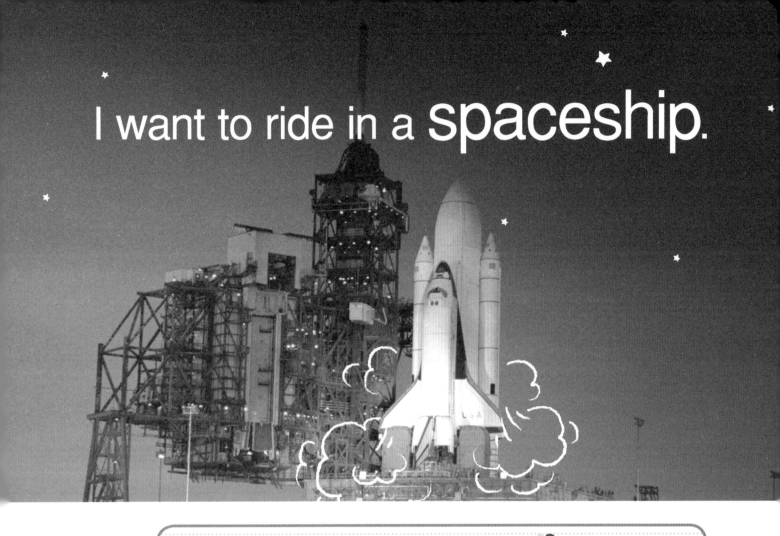

spaceship

spaceship

I Love Nature!

• Match the pictures with words!

leaf　　**flower**　　**tree**　　**island**　　**rock**

Write and Read

tree, flower, leaf, rock, cloud, island, forest ,
beach, river, canyon, mountain, desert, spring,
summer, fall, winter, sun, moon, star, earth

sun   star   earth   summer   spring

I love trees.

tree

Do you love trees?
Yes, I love trees.
Look at that tree on the hill!
Wow, it is huge and unique!

48

Flowers are beautiful.

A Little Talk

What beautiful flowers!

Yes, they are beautiful.

They are for you!

Thank you so much.

The **leaf** is green.

50

ROCKs are heavy.

A Little Talk

What are those?

They are rocks.

Why don't they move?

Because they are heavy.

Clouds look like cotton.

- What do you see?
- I see clouds in the sky.
- What do they look like?
- They look like cotton.

52

This is an island.

island

A Little Talk

Is that an island?

Yes, it is an island.

Is it a big island?

No, it is quite small.

Trees make forests.

54

A Little Talk

What are in the forests?

There are so many trees.

What else are in there?

Insects and animals!

Let's go to the **beach**.

beach beach

A Little Talk

Let's go to the beach.

What shall we do there?

We will swim and make sand castles.

This city has a **river.**

A Little Talk

Does this city have a river?

Yes, it does.

Can we tour along the river?

Of course we can.

I can see the **canyon.**

canyon

It is so high up here!

Be careful!

I can see the canyon.
It is big!

Yes, it is called
the Grand Canyon.

The **mountain**s have snow caps.

mountain

A Little Talk — Look at the mountains! Oh, wow! They are so high.

We are in the desert.

desert

desert

Where are we?
We are in the desert.
Can you see an oasis?
Not yet, but we will find one.

I love **spring**.

spring

spring

A Little Talk

I love spring!
Why do you love spring?
Because of all the flowers.
They are all pretty.

Summer is my favorite season.

summer

summer

A Little Talk

Do you like summer?

Yes, summer is my favorite season.

What do you like to do in summer?

I like to swim!

Fall is colorful.

fall   fall

A Little Talk

What happens in fall?
Leaves change colors
and fall off the trees.

It snows a lot in **winter.**

winter

winter

It is finally winter!

Yes, it snows a lot in winter.

Yay! It's snowing now!

Let's go out and have fun!

The **sun** is bright.

sun

64

A Little Talk

- What a beautiful day!
- I can't open my eyes.
- Yes, the sun is very bright.
- But it is so beautiful.

The **moon** has many shapes.

A Little Talk

What color is the moon?

It is yellow.

Does the moon have many shapes?

Yes, it changes every day.

moon

star | star

Do you like stars?

Yes, I like them so much.

What do you like about them?

The stars twinkle at night.

Earth is a beautiful planet.

earth

earth

I Want to Go Everywhere!

• Match the pictures with words!

house   restaurant   market   school   zoo

Write and Read

house, school, zoo, park, church, stadium, bookstore, theater, bakery, market, library, museum, hospital, playground, restaurant, kindergarten

| library | park | theater | hospital | playground |

Come into the house.

house house

A Little Talk

Where are you, dear?

I am out here, mom!

Come into the house.

Okay, I will, mom!

I go to **school.**

school

school

A Little Talk

It's time for school.

Yes, it's my first day of school.

Do you want to go to school?

Yes, I am excited.

The **ZOO** has many animals.

 Let's go to the zoo.

It's a wonderful idea!

The zoo has many animals.

I can't wait to see them.

ZOO ZOO

This is a nice **park.**

park | park

What a beautiful church!

church

church

Look at that building.
What is it?
It is a church.
What a beautiful church!

The **stadium** is so big.

Let's Go!

stadium

stadium

A Little Talk

👦 What is this stadium for?

👦 It is for a baseball game.

The **bookstore** is my favorite store.

bookstore

bookstore

A Little Talk — The bookstore is my favorite store. Let's go buy some book

The **theater** looks nice.

theater

theater

Movie

This is the new theater.

It looks nice! Shall we watch a play here?

Sure! Why not?

The **bakery** smells good.

bakery

bakery

A Little Talk

I'd like some bread.

There is a bakery.

Mmm, it smells so good.

Yes, it does. Let's go in.

78

I like going to the market.

market

market

A Little Talk

- I am going to the market.
- Can I come with you?
- Do you really want to?
- Yes, I like going to the market.

I read books in the **library**.

library

library

A Little Talk

What did you do yesterday?
I read books in the library.
What book did you read?
I read Three Little Pigs.

80

I learn a lot in **museum**s.

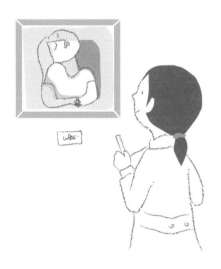

museum

museum

A Little Talk

- I learn a lot in museums.
- What do you learn?
- About art and history.
- Good for you!

A **hospital** is not a scary place.

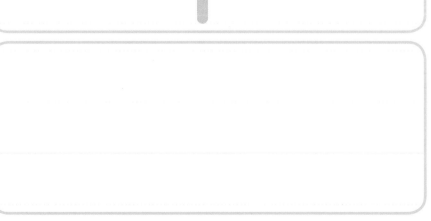

hospital

I feel very sick.
You need to go to hospital.
No! It is scary.
A hospital is not a scary place.

Have fun in the **playground**.

playground

playground

I'm at the **restaurant.**

restaurant

restaurant

A Little Talk — Can we eat out today? Okay. Let's go to a restaurant.

I love my kindergarten.

kindergarten

kindergarten

I Use Many Things!

Match the pictures with words!

bed   desk   mirror   drawer   couch

 ## Write and Read

bed, mirror, blanket, clock, couch, television, frame, telephone, toy box, computer, chair, desk, drawer, table, lamp, slippers, towel, toothbrush, soap, toilet

frame   television   clock   telephone   slippers

The **bed** looks nice.

A Little Talk

😊 Good morning, mom!
😊 Good morning, sweetie.
😊 I made my bed by myself.
😊 Good job! The bed looks nice!

bed bed

I look at myself in the **mirror.**

What's that?

It's a mirror.

What do you need it for?

I look at myself in the mirror.

89

Come under the blanket.

blanket

Isn't it chilly today?

Yes, it is quite cold.

Come under the blanket.

Okay!

90

There is a **clock** right there.

clock

clock

What is the time?

There is a clock right there.

Can you read it?

Yes, it is almost 2:10.

It's a comfortable couch.

couch

A Little Talk

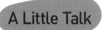 Can I sit on the couch?

Finish your meal first.

Well, the couch is so comfortable.

But you can't eat there.

My favorite show is on **television**.

television

television

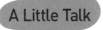
Time's up! Turn off the television.   Oh, no! My favorite show is on.

They are my pictures in the **frame**s.

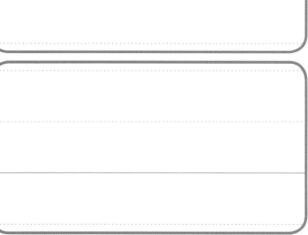

A Little Talk

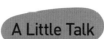 I put a picture in the frame.

Who is this?

It is you when you were a baby.

The **telephone** is ringing.

telephone

telephone

The telephone is ringing! Can you get it?

Yes, I'll get it.

Put your toys in the **toy box.**

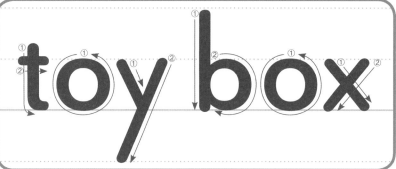

A Little Talk

👦 I am done playing, mom.

👩 Put your toys back where they were.

👦 In the toy box?

👩 Yes! Put them in the toy box.

May I use the computer?

computer

computer

A Little Talk

May I use
the computer?
Yes, go ahead.

Please sit on the chair.

chair

chair

A Little Talk

Please sit on the chair.

Why, dear?

I want you to rest for a little bit.

Oh, thank you.

98

I will study at my desk.

desk

A Little Talk

I need a new desk.

No, your desk is still fine.

Can I get a new one next year?

Yes, if you are good.

Can you organize your drawers?

drawer

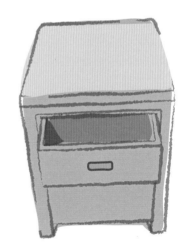

100

I read at the **table**.

table

table

A Little Talk

- The room looks clean and neat!
- I cleaned the table, mom.
- Did you? You did a good job!
- Thank you!

101

Read under the **lamp.**

lamp

lamp

102

A Little Talk

I want to read a book, mom.

It's too dark.

Do I need a lamp?

Yes, read under the lamp.

These **slippers** are really cute!

slippers

slippers

I made you some slippers.
Wow! These slippers are really cute.
Can I try them on?
Yes. Go ahead.

103

Can I have a clean **towel**?

towel   towel

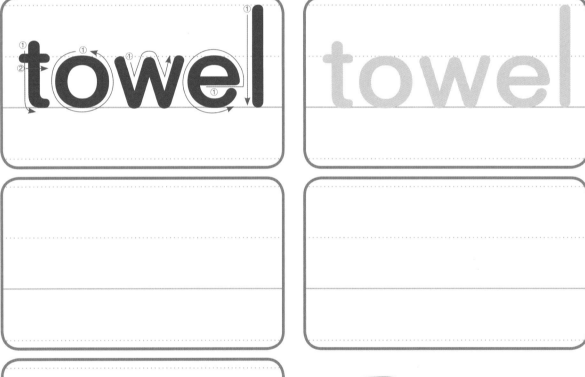

A Little Talk

👦 I am going to take a shower.
👩 What do you need?
👦 Can I have a clean towel?
👩 Sure. Here it is.

104

I have a pink **toothbrush.**

toothbrush

toothbrush

A Little Talk

Which toothbrush is yours?   Mine is pink. I'll brush my teeth now.   105

Use soap when you wash your hands.

soap soap

A Little Talk

My hands are dirty.
Go wash your hands.
Use soap when you wash.
Okay, I will.

Keep the **toilet** clean.

toilet

toilet

A Little Talk

- What is this?
- I took too much toilet paper.
  I am sorry. I will clean it.
- Make sure you keep the toilet clean.

Let's Play!

- Match the pictures with words!

piano   harmonica   flute   guitar   violin

Write and Read

piano, flute, violin, guitar, cello, drum, harmonica, xylophone, golf, soccer, ice hockey, bowling, skiing, baseball, basketball, swimming, tennis, marathon

soccer   golf   skiing   basketball   tennis

I can play the **piano**.

What instrument can you play?
I can play the piano.
Please play for me.
Sure!

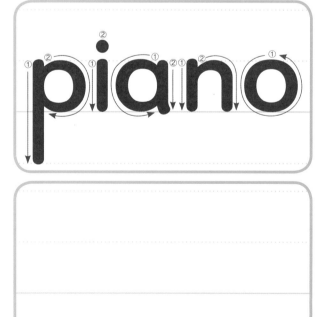

I am a **flute** player.

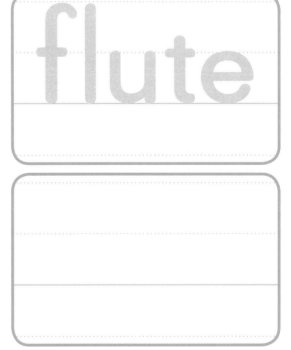

Did you practice the flute today?

Yes, I did. Listen!

You are very talented!

Thank you so much.

flute

Violins make a beautiful sound.

violin

A Little Talk

What are you playing?

I am playing the violin.

Violins make a beautiful sound.

I think so, too.

My guitar is my best friend.

guitar

guitar

A Little Talk

- Who is your best friend?
- Actually this guitar is my best friend.
  I play it all the time.

I did my **cello** practice.

cello

cello

👧 What did you do, sweetie? 👧 I did my cello practice.

Everybody loves the drums.

A Little Talk

Who wants to play the drums?

I do! I do!

Everybody loves the drums!

Yes, including me!

I play the **harmonica.**

harmonica

harmonica

A Little Talk 👦 Mom, I can play the harmonica. 👧 Really? Please play it.

I bought a new **xylophone**.

xylophone

xylophone

 I bought a new xylophone for you!  Yay! You are the best!

We play golf.

golf

golf

How was playing golf with your dad?   It was fun!

I am the best **soccer** player.

soccer

soccer

A Little Talk

See how I kick the ball!

Wonderful!

Who is the best soccer player?

Of course, you are!

119

Swing the ice hockey stick!

ice hockey

ice hockey

A Little Talk   I want to score.   Swing your ice hockey stick.

I'll win the
bowling game.

bowling

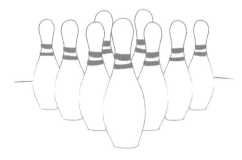

A Little Talk

- I'll win this bowling game.
- There goes the ball!
- Strike!
- You won the game!

I love the speed of skiing.

skiing

skiing

A Little Talk

- I love the speed of skiing.
- I do too, but please be careful.
- Don't worry.

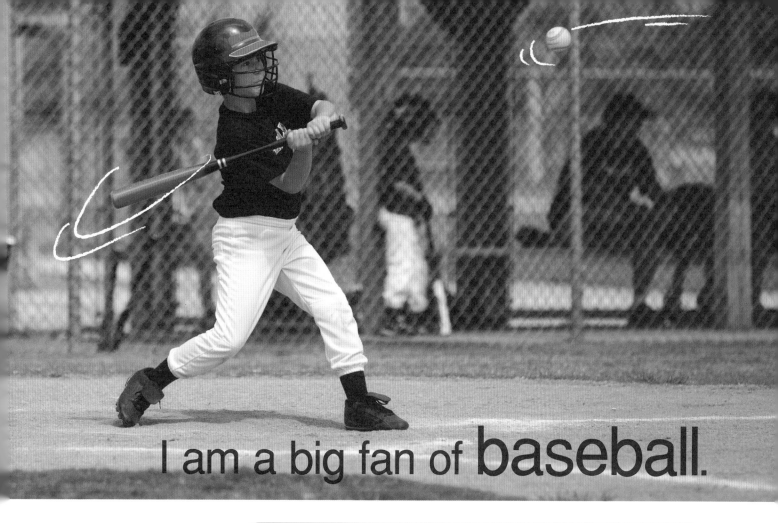

I am a big fan of **baseball.**

baseball

baseball

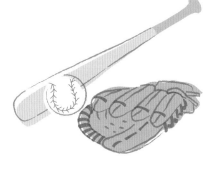

A Little Talk

😊 I'm a big fan of baseball.　😊 I am, too! Let's play it together sometime.　123

We love to play basketball

basketball

basketball

A Little Talk — My favorite sport is basketball. It's my favorite, too!

I enjoy swimming!

swimming

swimming

😊 What do you enjoy doing in summer?   😊 I enjoy swimming.   125

When did you start to play tennis?

tennis

tennis

A Little Talk

When did you start to play tennis

I started last week.

How do you like it?

I enjoy it so much.

I run a **marathon** every month.

marathon

marathon

 A Little Talk

I run a marathon every month.   Maybe you will win a race someday.   127

Index